G000271041

WAR AND PEACE

THE EPIC MASTERPIECE IN ONE SITTING

Summary by
JOELLE HERR

RUNNING PRESS
PHILADELPHIA · LONDON

9 8 7 6 5 4 3 2 1
Digit on the right indicates the number of this printing
Library of Congress Control Number: 2014941233
ISBN 978-0-7624-4845-6

Running Press Book Publishers
A Member of the Perseus Books Group
2300 Chestnut Street
Philadelphia, PA 19103-4371

Visit us on the web!
www.runningpress.com

CONTENTS

Introduction 5

The Life of Leo Tolstoy 11

War and Peace 30

A Note on the Text 31

Who's Who 33

Book I 52

Book II 94

Book III 158

Book IV 223

Epilogue 276

INTRODUCTION

Not only is *War and Peace* one of the longest novels ever written, but it's also one of the most universally revered—many proclaiming it *the* best novel, period. It has influenced the likes of such greats as Mahatma Gandhi, Martin Luther King Jr., and Nelson

NAPOLEON ON THE BATTLEFIELD AT BORODINO

Mandela, who wrote that, while unjustly imprisoned for twenty-seven years, "One book that I returned to many times was Tolstoy's great work, *War and Peace.*"

So, what's all of the hubbub about? Tolstoy's account of the tumultuous Napoleonic Wars—as experienced by four aristocratic Russian families—is a masterpiece for so many reasons. Perhaps most importantly, the book is an insightful look into the heart of a nation, and, indeed, Tolstoy has been referred to as "the guardian of Russia's soul." Even though he employed a third-person narrator, Tolstoy's sprinkling of "we" and "our" throughout the book created an indelible connection between the author and readers—Russian readers, in particular.

Even beyond that, though, there is universality in Tolstoy's words. German writer Thomas Mann said, "To read him . . . is to find one's way home . . . to everything within us that is fundamental and sane."

Although you're just one sitting away from having "read" one of the greatest novels ever written, I would be remiss if I didn't encourage you to read the real thing someday. The hubbub is completely warranted. For now, though, get ready to be transported back to early nineteenth-century Russia, where you'll mingle with the most elite members of society and follow them through tragedy and triumph over the course of fifteen years. Though you'll venture far and wide, as Mann attests, you'll find yourself back home at the end, richer and wiser from the journey.

THE LIFE
∾ of ∾
LEO TOLSTOY

L EO NICOLAYEVICH TOLSTOY
was born on September 9,
1828, at his aristocratic family's rural
estate, Yasnaya Polyana ("Bright
Glade"), situated 130 miles south
of Moscow, in the Tula region.

TOLSTOY AT TWENTY-NINE, AS AN OFFICER
IN THE CRIMEAN WAR

His family was very, very wealthy. When his parents married in 1822, his mother's dowry included a mind-boggling 800 male serfs.

Though privileged, Tolstoy's childhood was filled with death. His mother passed away when he was just one year old, his father dying of "apoplexy" when Tolstoy was nine. He and his four siblings—three brothers and one sister—were raised at Yasnaya Polyana by various extended family members (many of whom also died during Tolstoy's childhood) and educated at home.

In 1845, Tolstoy enrolled at Kazan University to study law and "Oriental languages." He was a horrible, undisciplined student and left before graduating.

Tolstoy inherited his share of his family's estate—which included 4,000 acres of Yasnaya Polyana and 350 serfs—in 1847. He spent the following years living between St. Petersburg, Moscow, and Yasnaya Polyana, developing a nasty gambling habit. He gambled away a lot of his wealth, incurring debts that had to be paid by selling off parts of Yasnaya Polyana. Another of his debaucheries involved bedding numerous peasant women, often.

In 1851, Tolstoy joined the army, stationed in Caucasus and eventually serving in the Crimean War, an experience that directly inspired *War and Peace*. It was during his service that his first works—novellas and stories—were published.

Weary of his addiction to gambling and women, Tolstoy began envisioning a more ascetic life—planting the seeds for the existential crisis he would have twenty years later. More immediate were a couple of attempts at social activism, including the 1859 establishment of a school to educate the children of his serfs.

After his military experience, Tolstoy traveled Europe, eventually winding up back in Moscow, where he met Sofya (called Sonya) Bers, who was from an enormously wealthy family that lived in the Kremlin. At the time of their marriage in 1862, Tolstoy was 34, Sonya only 18.

Perhaps setting the stage for the eventual dysfunction of their marriage, Tolstoy made Sonya read his diaries detailing the debauched escapades of his twenties, which included the fact that he had fathered an illegitimate son with a serf. Sonya was understandably scarred but apparently forgave her new husband for his cruel infliction. That said, they did, from time to time over the years, read each other's diaries, resulting in huge rows and lingering jealousies.

By all accounts, the early days of their marriage were happy ones, with Sonya giving birth to thirteen children over the course of twenty-five years. Eight of these children survived childhood.

Tolstoy continued to write during this time, chiefly on what would become *War and Peace*. Parts of the novel were serialized between 1865 and 1867, thoroughly captivating readers. When it was published in its entirety for the first time in 1869, it sold out nearly immediately. Critics, on the other hand, weren't quite sure what to make of the groundbreaking epic, though it didn't take long for them to come around and proclaim it a masterpiece.

Tolstoy's second masterpiece, *Anna Karenina*, began appearing in serial form in 1873. Fellow Russian writer Fydor Dostoyevsky proclaimed it "flawless as a work of art," and it sold about a zillion copies.

Shortly after the publication of *Anna Karenina*, though, Tolstoy began struggling with bouts of depression, futility, and self-doubt—even suicidal thoughts. He found some peace in the company of peasants, even working in the fields alongside his serfs. He started studying ancient Greek and apprenticed to a boot maker. He became increasingly moody and irascible—very difficult to live with. Poor Sonya tried to keep the household running smoothly.

In 1879, he published *A Confession*, which documented his

existential crisis and articulated his belief that true meaning and satisfaction could be attained through denouncing his aristocratic ways of life and devoting himself to the fundamentally Christian notion of helping the less fortunate. He gave up meat, hunting, smoking, and denounced his earlier works— even attempting to put them in the public domain.

The fact is that, while making these public declarations, Tolstoy continued to enjoy many comforts of his aristocratic life—a hypocrisy that he seemed oblivious to but that rankled many around him, including Sonya. He preached the benefits of abstinence—even within marriage—but didn't practice it himself. That said, his pacifism and benevolence did improve the lives of countless Russians.

As you can imagine, Tolstoy's newfound radical beliefs caused

increasing discord in his marriage, with Sonya struggling to keep the household running and protect his legacy. Though he had mostly turned his back on writing fiction, Tolstoy did write the illuminating novella, *The Kreutzer Sonata* (1889), in which a husband resembling Tolstoy murders a wife resembling Sonya. *Ouch.*

Influenced by Tolstoy's essays promoting his new world vision, others began to subscribe to Tolstoy's beliefs, making him a religious figure of sorts. His most loyal disciple was a fellow aristocrat named Vladimir Chertkov. Although Tolstoy was eventually excommunicated from the Russian Orthodox Church in 1901, he was never actually punished for his blasphemy—even though many of his followers, "Tolstoyans," were exiled to Siberia.

As the years passed, the relationship between Tolstoy and Sonya

deteriorated exponentially, with Chertkov wielding more and more power over Tolstoy's affairs.

On October 28, 1910, desperate to escape the constant conflict with Sonya, Tolstoy stole away from Yasnaya Polyana in the middle of the night, abandoning his home and forty-eight-year marriage. The eighty-two-year-old didn't make it far, however, before he fell ill with pneumonia at a

LEO AND SONYA TOLSTOY ON THEIR WEDDING ANNIVERSARY, SEPTEMBER 1910.

remote railway station in the town of Astapovo.

Upon hearing of his where-abouts and illness, Sonya rushed to his side. Tolstoy refused to see her, though, and she was kept waiting outside the station—along with scores of reporters chronicling the family drama and imminent death of one of the world's preeminent writers. At last, Sonya was allowed in to see her husband—but only after he had fallen into a coma, from which he never awoke.

Tolstoy passed away on November 7, 1910, and was buried on the grounds of Yasnaya Polyana, which miraculously survived the Russian Revolution of 1917 and has been preserved as a museum visited by thousands of Tolstoy acolytes every year. It's also the site of a massive Tolstoy family reunion every other year.

WAR
AND
PEACE

A NOTE ON THE TEXT

Unless fluent in Russian, anyone who decides to pick up
War and Peace is going to end up
reading a translation. Of course,
there are many different translations
out there, some better regarded than
others and each featuring a seemingly endless variance of character
name spellings. (*Andrey* vs. *Andrei*.
Marya vs. *Marie* vs. *Mary*. You get
the idea.) Left in most translations is

the abundance of French,
which was commonly spoken by
the aristocratic class back in early
nineteenth-century Russia.

WHO'S WHO

SINCE THE NOVEL clocks in at around 1,450 pages, it may not be terribly surprising that it features more than 500 characters! There's no need to get your head in a spin over that number, though, because the bulk of the action concerns the members of four aristocratic families—the Bezukhovs, the Kuragins, the Rostovs, and the Bolkonskys.

Here are some brief descriptions—physical and otherwise—of the most prominent characters.

THE BEZUKHOVS

Count Bezukhov—A very handsome, fabulously wealthy dandy from Catherine the Great's day. At the onset of the novel, he's retired to a country estate, living a life in seclusion and no longer participating in society.

Pierre—The illegitimate, sensitive, intellectual son of Count Bezukhov: "a stout and heavily built young man with close cropped hair and spectacles, wearing the light-colored breeches fashionable at the time, a brown dress coat, and a high jabot." Kind and good-hearted; his father's favorite child.

THE KURAGINS

Prince Vasily Kuragin—Fifty-something aristocrat who's bored with the duties that come along with his position in society: "He came in wearing his embroidered court uniform, knee breeches, and low shoes, with stars on his breast and a serene expression on his flat face." He has three children: daughter Ellen and sons Ippolit and Anatol.

Ellen Kuragin—"So lovely that not only did she show no trace of coquetry, but, on the contrary, appeared to be almost embarrassed by her undeniable, irresistible, and enthralling beauty." She's as ruthless and amoral as she is beautiful.

Ippolit Kuragin—"His face was overcast by an idiotic and invariably peevish, conceited expression, and his body was thin and weak. His eyes, nose, and mouth all seemed to be puckered into a vacant, bored grimace." Neither bright nor kind nor attractive.

Anatol Kuragin—"An attractive young man with bland features and gracious manners who evidently considered himself a celebrity, but, out of politeness, modestly placed himself at the disposal of the company in which he found himself." A grade-A pleasure seeker if ever there were one. Womanizing and spending his father's money are his hobbies.

THE ROSTOVS

Count Rostov—"Plump and jolly," this portly gentleman lives well and loves his family. Too bad he's not very good with finances.

Countess Natalya Rostov—"A woman of about forty-five, with a thin, Oriental-type of face, who looked worn out from childbearing; she had given birth to twelve." Her children and their happiness mean everything to her.

Vera Rostov—The oldest of the Rostov children and very openly not the favorite of her mother.

Nikolai Rostov—At the opening of the novel, he is still a student, a "short, curly-headed young man with an open expression." He and Sonya are childhood sweethearts.

Natalya "Natasha" Rostov—"Not pretty but full of life, with her black eyes and wide mouth," Natasha is only 13 years old at the opening of the novel. She is very bratty in a childish way, prone to whims and with very romantic notions. Her enthusiasm for everything lights up a room and draws all eyes to her. Just about every male in the book—save her family members—courts her at one point or another.

Petya Rostov—The youngest child, an eager, enthusiastic boy who's very close with his sister, Natasha.

Sonya Rostov—A poor cousin raised among the Rostov children. She's been in love with Nikolai as long as she can remember.

THE BOLKONSKYS

Prince Nikolai Bolkonsky—A crotchety old man described as "sharp and invariably demanding, so that, without being cruel, he inspired a degree of awe and respect that even the most obdurate of men would not have aroused."

Andrei Bolkonsky—The prince's son, a very handsome young man who's so miserable in his life that he decides that going to war is more appealing than the status quo: "Everything about him, from his weary, jaded aspect to his slow, measured step, was in the sharpest contrast to his vivacious little wife [Lisa]."

Lisa Bolkonsky—Andrei's sweet, beautiful, and much-admired wife. Too bad she's superficial and daft and Andrei can't stand being around her.

Nikolenka Bolkonsky—Andrei and Lisa's son. To say more would involve some massive spoilers.

Marya Bolkonsky—Andrei's unattractive sister, who's pretty much a saint in her patience and dedication and sincere care for others. Her eyes, "large, deep, and luminous (at times rays of warm light seemed to radiate from them), were really so beautiful that very often, in spite of the plain-

ness of her face, they gave her an
allure greater than beauty."

OTHERS

Princess Anna Mikhailovna—A
member of the nobility whose
wealth is long-gone. Everything she
does is for the improvement of her
beloved son, Boris.

Boris Mikhailovna—An officer:
"tall and fair, with delicate, regular

features and a look of composure on his handsome face." Son of Princess Anna, who is of an old, respected—though now penniless—family. A good friend of Nikolai Rostov and childhood sweetheart of Natasha Rostov.

Dolokhov—Good-for-nothing friend of Anatol Kuragin who loves cheating at cards and exacting cruelty on his enemies.

Lieutenant Berg—A young German opportunist—"irreproachably scrubbed, brushed, and buttoned up"—who ends up marrying Vera Rostov. He distinguishes himself in the military.

Kutuzov—Commander in Chief of the Russian Army. Tolstoy spends a lot of time analyzing his actions (and inactions) during the Napoleonic Wars, most notably questioning why he is criticized and Napoleon is continually called "grand" and "genius"; one thing's for sure, Kutuzov's job is his life. His country and its people mean everything to him.

Denisov—A good-hearted captain who serves with (and acts as mentor to) Nikolai. He's described as "a small, red-faced man with sparkling black eyes, tousled black hair and moustache." Incapable of pronouncing the letter "r."

Russian Tsar Alexander—Not a central character, as far as the action goes; he's pretty much just a figurehead, with little actual involvement in the wars.

Napoleon—Surely this fella needs no introduction. Here's Tolstoy's physical description of the man who has a whole complex named after him: "The whole of his short, corpulent figure, with the broad, thick shoulders and the chest and

stomach involuntarily thrust forward, had that imposing, stately
appearance common in men of
forty who live a life of comfort."

Platon Karatayev—Ah, Platon;
he's one of the most revered characters in all of Tolstoy's works.
Serene, kind, thoughtful, not a sin-
gle bad bone in his body.

❧ BOOK I ❧

I'T'S A JULY EVENING in Petersburg, and the vivacious Anna Pavlovna is throwing a grand soiree, at which the crème of the Russian social elite will be making their appearances and no doubt discussing the looming threat that is Napoleon Bonaparte.

First to arrive is Prince Vasily Kuragin. He and Anna discuss the prince's children, including his two sons, Ippolit and Anatol, the latter a reputed rogue. Anna suggests Princess Marya Bolkonsky—daughter of a very wealthy, clever-but-difficult retired military commander—as a suitable match for Anatol and promises to speak to Lisa, the princess' sister-in-law (the pregnant wife of Marya's brother, Andrei), who's expected at the party that evening.

Phew. That's a lot of names already in just the first couple of paragraphs! You still with me? OK, let's keep going.

Vasily's beautiful daughter, Ellen, arrives, along with her brothers, Ippolit and Anatol, followed by the uncouth Pierre, illegitimate son of Count Bezukhov, an old wealthy "grandee of Empress Catherine's time, who now lay dying in Moscow."

Pierre has recently returned from being educated abroad and has been been staying with Vasily for the past month. As this is his first Russian soiree, Pierre acts like "a child in a toyshop" (*seriously, that's Tolstoy's description!*) amid all of the clever and intelligent conversations swirling around the soiree.

Andrei Bolkonsky arrives next, seemingly bored to death by the idea of another party, and especially his wife. He's very relieved to see Pierre, his BFF, across the room. Hold up, though: everyone—Pierre in particular—gasps at the loveliness of Princess Ellen as she gets up to leave.

Talk, once again, returns to Napoleon. Anna recoils at Pierre's audacity when he dares defend the emperor, claiming that "the great man" brought order to France after the revolution. Amid all of the clamor of disagreement, Andrei chimes in to support his friend.

As the party breaks up, Anatol makes kind of a ninny of himself, flirting with the very married and very pregnant Lisa, right in front

of her husband, Andrei, who fortunately doesn't care one whit.

After the party, Andrei and
Pierre have a private pow-wow in
which Pierre admits that, since
Russia's freedom is not the point,
he is philosophically opposed to
joining the war against Napoleon.

Andrei reveals that he's decided
to go off to war because he's disen-
chanted with the emptiness of his
life (and wife). He advises Pierre to
never marry, or to at least wait until

he is old and has done everything he wants to do in life—and advises him to stop hanging around with the Kuragin boys, Ippolit and Anatol, who care about nothing but wine and women.

Despite promising not to, Pierre leaves Andrei's house and heads to join Anatol and his friends for a night of drunken debauchery. *Tsk, tsk.*

THE SCENE SHIFTS to Moscow and the Rostov family. Countess Natalya Rostov and her youngest daughter (also named Natalya but called Natasha) are receiving guests in honor of their name day (a Russian tradition).

There is gossip about a recent scandal involving Anatol, Pierre, and a fellow rabble-rouser named Dolokhov that's something right out of *The Hangover*: a drunken prank that included putting a bear in a carriage and sending it to a bunch of actresses. When a policeman tried to stop them, they tied him to the bear and pushed both into a canal. *Yes, you read that right.*

The discussion turns to the fact that, once Count Bezukhov dies (which is supposed to be imminent), it's unknown whether Pierre (his illegitimate son) or Vasily (related to the count through his wife) will inherit his huge estate, which includes 40,000 serfs!

Count Rostov's older son, Nikolai, has decided to leave university
and follow his friend, Boris, into
the military, the Russian army.
Boris—thanks to a recommendation
wrangled from Prince Vasily by Boris'
mother—will be an officer, while
Nikolai wants to join as a cadet.

Nikolai is in love with Sonya, his
cousin, while Boris is in love with
Natasha. When Natasha tries to
kiss him, Boris pushes her away but
promises to ask for her hand in four

years—when she's sixteen *(ahem)*.

In attendance at dinner that night are Boris and his mother, Anna, Pierre—who's been exiled to Moscow due to the bear incident—and a Lieutenant Berg, under whom Boris will be serving in the army. The talk, naturally, veers toward the recent declaration of war against the French and Napoleon.

After dinner—and a yummy-sounding dessert of pineapple ice

Illustration of NATASHA ROSTOV

cream—the guests play cards, and the young ones sing, and then there is dancing. Sonya has a bit of a meltdown, concerned that she and Nikolai won't be able to marry (since they are cousins) and worried that he will marry fellow guest Julie Karagina, who sat next to him at dinner. Natasha tries to comfort her cousin and tells her not to worry.

ON THE SAME EVENING as the dinner, Count Bezukhov suffers yet another stroke, and there appears to be no hope of recovery.

Vasily, in speaking to his cousin, Katish, reveals his knowledge of the fact that Bezukhov's will names Pierre as the sole beneficiary. Normally, this wouldn't matter, because, since Pierre is illegitimate, he would not legally be able to inherit. However, Vasily is worried that Bezukhov may have petitioned the Tsar for Pierre to be recognized, which would leave Vasily—and Katish—out in the cold.

Vasily asks Katish if she knows of such a letter's existence, suggesting, if so, that she destroy it before it reaches the Tsar. After some protest, she finally reveals the location of the will: in a folder under the dying count's pillow!

Pierre, hearing about his father's stroke, returns home, accompanied by the scheming Anna Mikhailovna, who goads him to "be a man" and "look after his interests."

Pierre, Anna, Vasily, and his young cousins (including Katish) join doctors in the count's room as clergymen perform the last anointment. At some point, Katish manages to swipe the folder, but not without Anna seeing it. After they leave the count to rest for a while, Anna and Katish actually physically struggle

over the folder, neither wanting
to let go of it. The count passes
away. No one yet knows the con-
tents of his will.

❧

IT IS AUTUMN at Bald Hills,
the Bolkonsky family's country
estate, about 100 miles outside of
Moscow. The old prince has long
since retired from the military,
living at Bald Hills full-time with
his daughter, Princess Marya.

A letter arrives for Marya from her BFF, Julie—the very same Julie that Sonya was so jealous of at the Rostovs' dinner party. In the letter, Julie relates the latest news from Moscow, which of course, revolves around the war. Julie rues the fact that she and Nikolai Rostov will likely never be more than friends, due to his being younger than she is.

Julie also confirms that Pierre has, indeed, inherited all of his father's great wealth, Vasily, Katish, and her sisters receiving next to nothing. This development has made Pierre Moscow's most eligible bachelor, and Julie's own mother has expressed the desire to match her with him—something Julie absolutely does not want.

Finally, Julie's letter mentions Anna Mikhailovna's intention to match Marya with Anatol, relating that all Julie knows of the young man is that he's "very handsome and terribly wild."

Marya writes back to Julie, protesting that she's known Pierre her whole life and that he has nothing but a kind heart. She says she feels sorry for him, being burdened with this great wealth. As to the matter of Anatol, Marya shares her devout view of marriage as a duty, claiming she'll be a devoted wife to whomever is chosen for her.

Prince Andrei and wife Lisa arrive at Bald Hills for a brief visit before he heads off to the war. Lisa will remain there while he's away. At dinner that evening, the discussion turns to . . . you guessed it, Napoleon.

Before Andrei leaves the next day, Marya gives him a religious trinket, one that their father and grandfather had both taken to war—and returned. She makes him promise to never take it off, and he agrees, despite his skepticism in anything relating to the mystical.

Andrei says his goodbyes, after which, "from the study, like pistol shots, came the repeated sound of the old Prince furiously blowing his nose." Andrei—much like a prisoner being released—is super thankful for his newfound freedom.

IT'S OCTOBER OF 1805, and the scene is Austria, where the Russian troops are encamped. Prince Andrei has taken his position as adjutant to Commander in Chief of the Russian army (that's the top guy, folks) Kutuzov. Word arrives of a recent brutal defeat of the Austrians by the French.

Meanwhile, cadet Nikolai Rostov is stationed nearby, serving under Captain Denisov, who's unable to pronounce the letter "r" and has a heavy gambling habit. The two share quarters and have become friends.

Nikolai gets into a bit of hot water after calling a superior a liar in front of the regiment and, with his rigid sense of right and wrong, refuses to apologize. The matter is dropped when word arrives of the Austrians' defeat, and everyone prepares to march to the front the next day.

The French are advancing upon Denisov and his men, who are bringing up the rear of the Russian troops. Denisov receives orders to burn a bridge after all of his men have crossed, in order to halt the French. Before they can light the bridge, they come under French fire. Nikolai panics and freezes, but no one notices in the commotion. They burn the bridge and return to the rest of the Russian troops.

The Russians—numbering around 35,000—are vastly out-numbered by the 100,000 French troops, and soon the Russians find themselves in a hasty retreat. Still, the Russians manage to defeat the French in a key battle, raising their spirits.

Andrei is sent to inform the Austrian Emperor Franz of the victory.

On his ride, he feels alive, like his life finally has meaning and purpose. His mood is ruined upon his arrival by the seeming indifference that meets his news and the disappointment that no high-level French commanders were captured or killed in the battle. Andrei learns that the French have taken over Vienna, one explanation for the Austrian Minister of War's grumpiness.

Prince Andrei—with rather grand illusions of becoming a

hero—returns to the Russian troops, who are in sorry shape—exhausted, demoralized, hungry, low on supplies, and low in numbers—and retreating.

One small squadron, commanded by Prince Bagration, is left behind to fend off the French (now numbering 150,000), while the rest of the Russian forces await additional supplies and reinforcements.

After practically begging Kutuzov to let him go, Andrei joins

Bagration's tiny squadron of 4,000 men. Andrei explores the camp, and when he reaches the front, he overhears some of the Russian men jokily talking smack with French soldiers across the enemy line— that's how close the two camps are to each other. *Ah, the grand old days of "civilized" war between gentlemen.*

Soon, the French launch a strike. The great battle has begun, and before long, the Russians are retreating.

We witness the conflict unfold through Andrei, who's shadowing Bagration. Even though he should be terrified (and probably is), Andrei is still completely energized by what's going on around him: He feels truly alive and contented. Still, chaos quickly ensues, with soldiers running willy-nilly. Suddenly, though, the French fall back, which allows the Russians a little time to regroup. Later, all of the officers report to Bagration their accounts of the battle, after which Andrei first starts to feel an inkling of disillusionment with the war.

❧❧

SO, PRINCE VASILY: Turns out he's a bit of a schemer, with "not merely one or two such plans and schemes under way, but dozens." One of his latest ideas is to get the recently legitimized and extremely wealthy Pierre—the new Count Bezukhov—to marry his daughter, Ellen, so that he can have access to the Bezukhov fortune. To this purpose, Vasily takes Pierre under his wing, guiding him through society, which, now that he's inherited, now welcomes Pierre with open arms.

For his part, Pierre is feeling overwhelmed by his new position. So many balls and dinners and people wanting to speak with him and laugh at his jokes—even Anna Pavlovna has changed her tune, gushing over him. For his part, Pierre is both enchanted by Ellen's beauty and repulsed by her apparent shallowness, even recalling a past rumor of there being some sort of scandalous affair between her and her brother, Anatol. (*Anyone else wondering if George R.R. Martin is a Tolstoy fan?*)

In the end, though, Pierre cannot resist Ellen's supremely alluring beauty. Six weeks later, they are married and settled in Petersburg.

IT'S DECEMBER OF 1805, and the scene shifts back to Bald Hills and the Bolkonsky family. Vasily goes to visit Prince Bolkonsky, bringing his son, Anatol. Remember, Vasily wants to get Anatol out of his hair, and Anna Pavlovna had suggested Bolkonsky's daughter, Marya, as a potential wife for him. The two have actually never met.

Unfortunately, despite her fancy dress and fashionable hairdo, when it comes right down to it, Marya is plain. We feel her anxiety as she's called to take tea with the man who may be her future husband. As she leaves her room, we learn that she has intense longing for "earthly love." Perhaps she and the scoundrel Anatol would be well suited for each other, after all?

Of course, Anatol is disappointed by Marya's lack of beauty, but he is intrigued by her pretty French companion, Mademoiselle Bourienne, who is, herself, taken by Anatol's handsomeness. Leaving her father's study after being informed of Anatol's desire to have her as his wife, Marya spies Anatol and Bourienne in an embrace. She turns down the proposal, resolute in her destiny to be a spinster and make others happy, even expressing a desire to facilitate a union between Anatol and Bourienne. *Can you say martyr complex?*

❧✦❧

NOVEMBER 12, 1805: It's back to the front. Nikolai Rostov has been injured in battle—or so the story goes. In reality, he has fallen off his horse and sprained his arm. In any case, he is promoted to an officer for his troubles.

December 2, 1805: The stage is set for the Battle of Austerlitz (also referred to as the Battle of the Three Emperors) between the French and Russians/Germans/Austrians, in which Napoleon himself will be leading his troops. The Russian Tsar Alexander I and Roman Emperor Francis II are also in attendance. Tolstoy's description of the night before the battle and then the battle—the battle cries, the building anticipation, the confusion among the thousands of troops—is simply magnificent. As the Russians advance, they realize that the French are much closer than they thought.

Andrei has his moment of glory, leading a charge against the enemy.

He is shot and, before losing consciousness, takes in the beautiful sky above ("How is it I did not see this sky before? How happy I am to have discovered it at last!"), finally feeling the peace and fulfillment he had so desperately been in search of.

Atop his horse, Nikolai charges through the commotion of the battle. He's been commissioned to deliver a message to Kutuzov and the Tsar. He passes Boris, who's exhilarated from fighting at the front. Suddenly Nikolai starts hearing shots coming from behind him. It appears the French are coming at them from the front and behind. It's not looking good.

Nikolai is desperate to deliver his message, but Kutuzov and the Tsar are not where they were supposed to be. He finally finds out that they had "bolted" (*Tolstoy's word!*) long before. Not really sure where to go, Nikolai just rides on, going down a road despite being warned that everyone who's gone down that road has been killed. He comes upon the Tsar, who's alone and looking confused. Nikolai debates whether to approach him but then decides to keep riding. He eventually changes his mind, but by the time he returns to where the Tsar was, he's gone.

Andrei regains consciousness, aware he's suffering from a horrible head wound. Napoleon himself walks by and notices that Andrei is not dead and orders his wound to be dressed. Unsurprisingly, Andrei feels an urgent appreciation for life and desire to go back home to Bald Hills, where his family, wife, and soon-to-be-born baby await him.

✤ BOOK II ✤

IT'S EARLY IN 1806. Nikolai Rostov goes home to Moscow on leave, bringing Denisov with him. Before he gets to the drawing room, where his family is, "something flew out of a side door like a tornado and began hugging and kissing him. Then a second and a third creature of the same order popped out of other doors and there was more hugging and kissing, more outcries, and tears of joy." Needless to say, his family is happy to see him!

Nikolai, naturally, feels more worldly and changed from his experience in the army. For one, he distances himself from Sonya. Even though she's beautiful and charming, he kind of wants to see what else is out there and sow some wild oats. Meanwhile, Denisov is succumbing to the charms of little Natasha.

Poor Pierre. Rumors are swirling that his wife—the former Ellen Kuragin—has been somehow "compromised" by Dolokhov (his former cohort in drinking, womanizing, and playing pranks— recall the officer tied to the bear). Naturally, Pierre is crushed.

Despite the stunning defeat of the Russians at Austerlitz, the returning soldiers are lauded by the public, who blame the Austrians for the loss. Count Rostov plans a banquet in honor of Prince Bagration. At the banquet, it becomes clear that Andrei is presumed dead. Pierre is there, looking all melancholy. As if the rumors swirling his wife weren't enough—he is seated across from none other than Dolokhov, himself.

After Dolokhov acts like a general ass during dinner, Pierre challenges him to a duel, in which Pierre ends up shooting Dolokhov in the side. Enraged with his wife, Pierre leaves Moscow for Petersburg, intending to never set eyes on her again.

IT'S TWO MONTHS after Austerlitz. Andrei is presumed dead, but Lisa has not been told because of the late stage of her pregnancy. She goes into labor, and a doctor is called for. That night, a carriage draws up to the house, but it's not the doctor—it's Andrei! He goes to see his wife, who's still in labor, but is quickly ushered out. Lisa dies giving birth to Andrei's son. *(Cue the violin music and the additional birth of Andrei's guilt.)*

TIME PASSES. Dolokhov recovers from the duel gunshot and rejoins society. Turns out he's fallen for young Sonya.

Talk turns to Napoleon and the war, and Nikolai plans to return to his regiment with Denisov after the Christmas holidays. Dolokhov proposes to Sonya, who turns him down. Nikolai tells Sonya that he loves her but cannot make any promises. He's young and still needs to date around. Sonya says nothing.

Before departing Moscow, Dolokhov invites Nikolai over to his hotel. Dolokhov is playing cards with some friends. After initially declining, Nikolai gives in to Dolokhov's peer pressure and plays. Hours later (and no doubt a hefty amount of cheating on Dolokhov's part), Nikolai is out an astounding 43,000 rubles. Nikolai promises to pay him the next day.

Returning home, Nikolai is mortified to have to ask his father for the money. The count appears to take it in stride, saying it happens to everyone at some point and that he's got the money. Denisov has proposed to Natasha, who's thrilled at the gesture but not in love with him.

It takes a couple of weeks for the count to raise all of the money, but he does. After paying the debt, Nikolai returns to his regiment in Poland at the end of November 1806.

AFTER THE RIDICULOUS DUEL,
Pierre leaves for Petersburg. On his
way, he encounters a Freemason, and
they have a philosophical discussion
in which Pierre admits he does not
believe in God, lamenting: "I abhor
my life."

Shortly after arriving in Petersburg, Pierre is invited into the
brotherhood of the Freemasons—
on the condition that he take back

his statement about not believing in God—and he accepts. He's taken to a huge house and goes through initiation. Afterward, he feels like a completely new man and departs to live on his estates in the south (near Kiev).

THE STORY THEN turns to Boris, who's attending one of Anna Pavlovna's soirees. There, he captures the attention of poor, abandoned-by-

her-husband Ellen, who asks him to
call on her sometime. Before long,
he's a regular visitor to her house. *(It
looks like there might have been truth
in those rumors after all!)*

PIERRE ARRIVES at his southern
estates, ordering his stewards to lib-
erate all of his serfs there and build
schools, hospitals, and churches
for them. Instead of embracing the
tenants of Freemasonry, though,

he falls into his old habits (*vices*) of partying and women.

In early 1807, on his way to Petersburg, Pierre stops at his various estates to gauge the progress of his orders, which he finds to be satisfactory, filling him with pride at improving the lives of these peasants. Little does he know that his stewards are putting on a show for him—that nothing has really changed.

Pierre decides to visit his old friend, Andrei, whom he hasn't seen in two years. Andrei is building a new house on one of his estates not far from Bald Hills. They have a philosophical discussion about whether what Pierre is doing with his serfs is actually making them better off. They agree to disagree on the matter. Pierre gushes to Andrei about the wonders of Freemasonry and how it has enriched his life. Andrei invites Pierre to dinner at Bald Hills, where he is met warmly by the old prince and Marya.

HIS LEAVE OVER, Nikolai returns to his regiment, including Denisov, who embraces him. It's good to be back. And a relief to be distanced from the complexities and stresses of back home—Sonya, the shame of losing so much money to Dolokhov.

It's April of 1807. Supplies for the men are in short supply. Denisov leaves the camp and comes back with provisions—that he intercepted. They were meant for another camp. He is court-martialed over the affair (which is technically theft), but before he can be tried, he is shot in the leg on patrol one day and is sent to a hospital for treatment.

Six weeks later, Nikolai goes to visit Denisov. The hospital is filled with sallow, emaciated men and the stench of rotting flesh and death. The state—and evident neglect—of the men is deeply distressing to Nikolai. Denisov is bitter about being called a robber but eventually, reluctantly, agrees to petition the Tsar for a pardon, asking Nikolai to deliver the request in person.

It's June, and Napoleon and Tsar Alexander have agreed to a truce. Boris is now one of the elite officers assigned to accompany the Tsar. Nikolai arrives with Denisov's petition and stops

in to see Boris, who welcomes
him with barely disguised annoy-
ance, and invites him to join his
dinner party, which includes two
French officers.

Nikolai still regards the French
as the enemy and is feeling quite
unwelcome and uncomfortable.
He asks Boris for help with Denisov's petition. When Boris recom-
mends not approaching the Tsar
directly, Nikolai gets annoyed and
basically says never mind.

On a whim and determined to help his friend, Nikolai goes to the house where the Tsar is staying. He tries to present the petition but is turned away for not going through the proper channels and not wearing his uniform. He runs into a cavalry general he once served under and spills the whole Denisov story. The general asks for the letter, but then the Tsar enters the room. The general goes to speak to him, after which the

Tsar announces there's nothing he can do for Denisov—"the law is mightier than I."

As Nikolai witnesses Napoleon and the Tsar publicly shaking hands and congratulating each other, he thinks back to the hospital where Denisov lay—with all of the stench and suffering and amputations—and wonders what in the world it was all for.

IN 1809, when France declares war on Austria, the Russians actually support their former enemy, the French. Andrei has spent the last couple of years pretty much isolated in the country, between Bald Hills (where his son is being raised) and his other estate. He's implemented some of Pierre's changes—freeing serfs and hiring midwives for pregnant peasants—and passed his time analyzing and writing a report on the failed Russian efforts against the French.

On a visit to the Rostovs' country estate for business, Andrei—like every other man who encounters her, it seems—becomes enchanted by the lovely Natasha. Her youthful exuberance and utter zest for life hit Andrei at his core. He stops feeling guilty for Lisa's death, realizes thirty-one is way too young to give up on life, and decides he is worthy of love and joy and all that sort of stuff. He goes back to Petersburg and rejoins society, where he is embraced and questioned about his decision to free his serfs.

Andrei's analysis of the Russian military is submitted for review, and as a result, Andrei is appointed to the Committee on Army Regulations. At a party one evening, Andrei makes the acquaintance of the Secretary of State, Speransky. They become fast friends, sharing the same views on

many things. Speransky also gets
Andrei appointed to the Commis-
sion for the Revision of the Legal
Code, where he will specialize in the
area of "Personal Rights."

SWITCH TO PIERRE. Disillusioned
with the state of Russia's Freemasons,
he goes abroad to see what fellow
brothers are up to. In 1809, he
returns to Petersburg, where he
urges his curious brothers that they

must change, must give up vices and devote themselves to "virtue." Some agree with him, but the majority of his brothers don't. When he's informed that his proposal will be rejected, he is disappointed and slips into a depression. He consults a friend, who urges him not to give up on his brothers.

Pierre also decides to reunite with his wife, Ellen, after two years apart—as a husband in name only, not in the bedroom. Once again,

Ellen becomes the crème of Petersburg society, throwing soirees and charming all of the attendees.

For his part, Pierre, thinking her quite vapid, stays out of her way, completely uninterested in the hubbub. He has sparks of jealousy—in particular regarding Boris—but he keeps his suspicions—and certain repeated heartbreak—at bay by not letting his wife into his heart . . . or his bed.

THE ROSTOVS are experiencing some serious financial difficulties, and so the elder count moves the family to Petersburg, where he seeks out a military appointment. Their frequent visitors include Pierre and Berg, the wounded veteran who's become engaged to the oldest Rostov countess, Vera. (At the age of twenty-four, she had not yet been proposed to and was well on her way to spinsterhood.) Only problem is that there's absolutely no money for a dowry. Unable to admit this, the elder Rostov promises 100,000 rubles, digging himself into further debt.

In 1809, Natasha is sixteen, the age at which she and Boris had agreed they would become engaged, a notion that she now brushes off as the whims of youth, especially since he hasn't been to visit them in years.

After the Rostovs move to Petersburg, though, Boris calls on them, with the intention of making it clear that there is no binding agreement between him and Natasha.

Of course, upon seeing her, he falls under her spell, despite telling himself that to marry her—him with no means and her family with no money—would be impossible. Still, he's drawn to her and so spends a lot of time at the Rostov house, making excuses to himself that he intends to make it clear that there's nothing between them. He even stops visiting Ellen, who chastises him with daily notes *(ahem)*.

Natasha is clearly still in love with Boris, though. Eventually, the countess has a talk with Boris and asks him to stop coming over—nothing can ever happen between him and Natasha. And so he stops visiting.

It's New Year's Eve, and a grand ball is being thrown in Petersburg—even the Tsar himself will be in attendance. It is Natasha's first ball. Everyone is there, including Pierre, Ellen, Andrei. The first dance begins. Pierre prompts Andrei to ask Natasha to dance. They are both very handsome and very good dancers. And of course: "he had no sooner put his arm around that slender, supple, quivering waist and felt her stirring so close to him and smiling up into his face, than her charm went to his head like wine." By the end of the night, he tells himself she won't be unattached for long.

At a dinner at Speransky's house, Andrei has an epiphany, suddenly seeing his work of the past four months on trying to reform military codes as utterly futile. The next day, he calls on the Rostovs. He may be in love with Natasha, but he funnels

the joy she awakens in him not to her but to his own life, deciding to make the most of it.

Andrei falls head over heels, deeply in love with Natasha and intends to ask for her hand. When he speaks of his plan to his father, the old prince frowns upon the match and advises his son to hold off on the marriage for a year and travel abroad. After some thought, Andrei decides to abide by his father's wish.

ANDREI BOLKONSKY AND NATASHA ROSTOV

Natasha is heartbroken when Andrei doesn't show up for a visit for three whole weeks, with no explanation. But then he shows up, letting her know that he was visiting his father. Andrei formally proposes to Natasha, saying that they will keep the engagement a secret so if she changes her mind in a year, she will be free to back out without social repercussions. She's disappointed that they must wait a year but sobs with happiness at the prospect of becoming his wife.

Marya is surprised when Andrei writes to her about the secret engagement. She doesn't think Natasha is worthy of her brother.

❧❧

MEANWHILE, NIKOLAI ROSTOV has taken over command of the squadron that was once Denisov's (whose fate is not yet revealed), living a peaceful, uncomplicated life. He dreads returning to his family, but a letter from his mother saying the family's possessions are about to be auctioned off prompts him to head to the Rostov estate in Otradnoe.

The financial affairs are indeed in a bad state. It's such an overwhelming mess that Nikolai can't deal with it. He decides to devote his efforts elsewhere—hunting.

It's September 15, 1810, and Nikolai is going hunting. His father, the old count, and Natasha decide to accompany him. The day winds down with the younger Rostovs visiting with "Uncle," a distant relative who lives nearby. There is music and singing and dancing and happiness. Nikolai hopes that Natasha will not marry Andrei in the end.

COUNT ROSTOV SELLS off a couple of estates, vowing to live more "simply," but their lifestyle is still quite lavish and expensive. The countess realizes that the family's only hope is for Nikolai to marry a wealthy heiress, specifically Julie Karagina. (Remember her from the dinner party years ago? If not, go to page 64 to refresh your memory.)

When the countess informs Nikolai of her idea, he responds that he wants to marry for love. He does not pursue Julie, and soon it's clear to his mother that he's still in love with Sonya.

Meanwhile, Natasha is getting restless. Andrei keeps delaying his return from abroad due to health reasons, leaving her feeling like she's wasting her time, whining like the immature child that she still is: "Worst of all, I am getting old."

It's the Christmas season, though, and during the celebrations, Nikolai's eyes are reopened to Sonya's beauty and charms, and he wonders how his heart could have ever strayed from her. One night, they share a secret, passionate kiss. Niko-lai confesses his feelings for Sonya to Natasha, who's thrilled at the news of her brother's reignited love for her best friend.

That night, the giggling girls (Natasha and Sonya) giddily gab about their men and decide to play a sort of game with a pair of mirrors that will reveal their futures. Sonya doesn't see anything in the mirrors, of course, but she pretends to see Andrei lying down in a bed.

Natasha wonders what this means, works herself up into a frenzy, and heads straight to bed.

Nikolai informs the countess of his intention to marry Sonya. She's not surprised by his declaration but lets her son know that neither she nor the count will give their blessing to this unfortunate pairing. Things get tense in the household. The countess takes out her frustration on Sonya, and the count blames himself and his messy financial affairs for the current woes. Nikolai leaves to tie up his military concerns, intending to marry Sonya upon his return.

The count must sell the Moscow townhouse in order to pay for Natasha's trousseau. For her part, Natasha is getting more and more embittered at having to wait for Andrei. Her interest is waning. At the end of January 1811, the count takes Sonya and Natasha to Moscow to handle the sale of the house

there. The countess remains behind
in the country.

PIERRE'S NOT FEELING so great
about things. Seeing his friend
Andrei so happy in his engagement
to Natasha has just reinforced the
emptiness of his own marriage and
way of living. He falls into his old
ways of drinking and carousing
and card playing, eventually leaving
Petersburg for Moscow: "In Mos-

cow he felt snug and at peace, as one feels in a shabby old dressing gown." There, he continues these habits— as well as a lot of reading—as a way to distract himself from the empti- ness, the hypocrisy, the injustices all around him.

MARYA AND HER FATHER leave Bald Hills to spend some time in Moscow. She doesn't care much for city life, not being invited to dinners or parties—and not wanting to go, anyway. Her brother's approaching marriage to Natasha is stressful, too, because their father is still opposed to it and cruelly taking his anger out on her. Making matters even worse is her father's increasing closeness to her French companion, Mademoiselle Bourienne.

Prince Bolkonsky has a new doctor, a Frenchman named Métivier, who comes to see him twice a week. On the morning of his name day, St. Nikolai's day, the prince pitches a tantrum, accusing the doctor of being a spy and then turning his wrath to his daughter for having let the doctor into the house. He blows up and finally orders Marya to move out—he can no longer live with her.

That night, at an intimate dinner, there is much discussion of Napoleon and another seemingly imminent war with the French. Boris and Pierre are both at the dinner, and afterward, Pierre pulls Marya aside and warns her that Boris has come to Moscow to find a wealthy wife, and has his sights set on her and Julie Karagina as contenders. Marya asks Pierre about her future sister-in-law, Natasha. The Rostovs are expected in Moscow shortly, as is Andrei.

Indeed, Boris has been paying special attention to Julie, who is receptive to his advances, expecting a proposal at some point. Boris cannot resign himself to marry for just money, though, and does not pop the question. When Anatol arrives in town, Boris finally snaps to, not wanting to be made a fool of and lose out on the prospect of marrying such a wealthy woman. He rushes over to Julie, at first quarreling with her, and then reluctantly proposing to her. Signs do not point to it being a happy marriage.

COUNT ROSTOV ARRIVES in Moscow with Sonya and Natasha. Andrei is due back from abroad at any moment. Natasha goes to visit Marya and her father, the prince. Even though she knows that the old prince is against her marriage to Andrei, Natasha isn't nervous about meeting him—after all, she's charmed everyone she's ever met. How could he possibly not adore her?

When Natasha and her father arrive at the Bolkonskys' house, the count refuses to see them. When Marya greets them, she instantly dislikes Natasha, thinking her vain and vapid. In return, Natasha thinks Marya is "ugly, affected, and unsympathetic." As their awkward conversation (or lack thereof) continues, the old count bursts into the room in his dressing gown—*awkward alert*—mumbling nonsense. Natasha can't get out of that house fast enough, inwardly cursing Andrei for taking so long to return and marry her.

❧❧

TIME FOR A NIGHT at the opera. Natasha is completely bored by the production, but the very dashing Anatol Kuragin does catch her eye—and she his. Also in attendance is Anatol's friend, the captivating Dolokhov—Sonya's onetime suitor and the man Nikolai had lost so much money to while playing cards—who's a hot commodity within high society. Assigned to a post in Persia, he's taken on their style and manner, which lend him a mysterious and exotic—and alluring to the ladies—air.

At one intermission, Ellen Bezukhov—the most beautiful woman in the whole theater—expresses interest in showing Sonya and Natasha around the town and invites Natasha to sit in her box so that they may get to know each other. Natasha is happy to bask in the glow of the attention of such a fine lady.

Of course, Ellen introduces Natasha to her brother, Anatol. Natasha is fascinated by him and his obvious enthrallment with her, but she also feels uncomfortable with the forwardness of his manner. He invites her to a costume "tournament," saying she will be the prettiest one there.

On the ride home, Natasha can think of nothing but Anatol—her intended, Andrei, the furthest thing from her mind. Later, she feels shame for having forgotten about Andrei and perhaps acting improperly with Anatol, but her thoughts keep returning to her dashing new acquaintance.

ANATOL IS IN MOSCOW, his father having sent him away from Petersburg for spending too much money. Prince Vasily has recommended either Julie or Marya as a suitable wife, but Anatol is more interested in gypsy women and French actresses. In fact, he is actually already a married man, having been coerced (*how or why, it's unclear*) to wed a Polish farmer's daughter (*presumably, Anatol had gotten her pregnant*)!

It wasn't long after the wedding, though, that he paid his father-in-law a certain settlement and abandoned his wife. Few know of these events—

to almost everyone, Anatol is still an eligible bachelor. For his part, Anatol seems incapable of reflection or remorse: "He believed that just as a duck had been created to live in water, so God had created him to spend thirty thousand a year and always to occupy a prominent position in society."

Anatol confides in Dolokhov his interest in Natasha, saying he means to pursue her. Dolokhov advises him to wait until she's married. Anatol ignores him, saying, "You know I adore little girls. They lose their heads at once." *What a complete rake!*

ELLEN INVITES SONYA and Natasha over to a gathering at her house. She is amused by the idea of throwing her brother and Natasha together and watching trouble brew. The count tries to keep an eye on his daughter the whole evening, but Anatol manages to profess his mad love for Natasha, leaving her confused as to whether she loves him or Andrei.

Anatol sends Natasha a love letter (penned by Dolokhov), gushing with love for her. This tips Natasha in favor of him over Andrei. Sonya finds the letter and, knowing Anatol is a scoundrel, confronts Natasha, who declares her undying and complete love for him, and he for her, saying she'll just, like, *die* without Anatol.

After a few days, Sonya deduces from Natasha's behavior that she's planning on running away with Anatol. Indeed, Anatol is planning an elopement, a "mock marriage," since he's already married, of course.

Fortunately, Sonya spills the beans to their hostess, who locks Natasha in her room and orders her servants to detain the two men (Anatol and Dolokhov) expected at the house that night. The elopement is thwarted, but Natasha is devastated and word of it spreads like wildfire. Pierre manages to force Anatol to leave town for Petersburg and swear to never, ever tell anyone what almost happened with Natasha.

Natasha is now out of the woods, but it turns out that she poisoned herself with some arsenic the night she was told of Anatol's marriage. She only took a little, though, and is fine. It was just a little cry for attention. No real harm done.

Andrei arrives in town, and Pierre goes to visit him. If Andrei is heartbroken, he's not showing it. In fact, he's clearly disgusted by the whole affair. When Pierre starts to suggest that Andrei marry Natasha nonetheless, Andrei cuts him off and says they must never speak of it again.

Pierre goes to see Natasha, who's in bad shape. He is so moved by her that his heart nearly bursts. He exclaims that if things were different, he would declare his own love for her and beg that she accept it. As he rides home afterward, he feels a new life blossoming, one in which he has no attachments.

Meanwhile, it's clear that another war with France is imminent.

ꙮ BOOK III ꙮ

ON JUNE 12 OF 1812, Russia is invaded: It's another war. The reasons are numerous, and Tolstoy doesn't refrain from pointing out that many of them don't make much sense—or at least don't warrant the "slaughter" of millions of men. But the war was fated.

The Tsar learns of Napoleon's invasion while at a ball. He writes a letter to Napoleon giving him a chance—practically begging him—to turn back without incident, though he's determined he'll never agree to peace until every last French troop is off his lawn . . . er, out of

Russia. He sends his Adjutant General, Balashev, to deliver the letter.

Balashev is finally granted an audience with Napoleon, who toys with him, whining that he doesn't *want* war but feels he's being *pushed* into it by the Tsar's actions (and alliances).

After tweaking (*that's tweaking, not twerking*) Balashev's ear ("To have one's ear tweaked by the Emperor was considered the greatest honor and mark of favor in the French

Court"), Napoleon sends Balashev back to the Tsar with a reply.

❧

BEFORE HE'S ABLE to track down Anatol and challenge him to a duel over the Natasha scandal, Andrei returns to the army, serving under Kutuzov in Turkey. On his way to joining the Western forces—at his own request—Andrei stops at Bald Hills to see his family, including his son, little Nikolenka. Things are as awkward as ever, with the old prince still conspiring with Mademoiselle Bourienne against Marya, treating her terribly. Andrei practically peels out of there, wondering what it's all worth. (Life, of course.)

Andrei attends a war council being held by the Tsar, which reminds him of the one he witnessed before Austerlitz, getting quite heated at times. After the meeting, Andrei requests to be sent to the front over remaining with the Tsar.

NIKOLAI ROSTOV RECEIVES
word from his parents of Natasha's
broken engagement—though he is
spared the details involving Anatol. He ignores their request that
he retire from the army and return
home. After responding to them
that he will see what he can do,
Nikolai writes a letter to Sonya,
expressing his love and devotion to
her, saying that he must fulfill his

duty to the army, but afterward, he will return to her, marry her, and devote his whole life to her happiness.

With impending battles ahead, Nikolai reflects that, though he's still afraid, it's not the same fear he felt at Austerlitz. Now he feels he's able to control his thoughts "in the face of danger."

Nikolai hears the familiar sound of far-off (but kind of near) gunfire. *Here we go again.*

With hardly any thought—other than seeing an opportunity to exploit a weakness in the French formation—Nikolai charges into the battle on his horse. He strikes down a young enemy officer from his horse. The young man looks frightened and immediately surrenders. He's taken prisoner, and Nikolai's conscience weighs heavy. The boy wasn't hostile but afraid. Nikolai is commended for his bravery, even getting his own squadron. None of it makes sense to him. Not at all.

❧

AFTER THE BROKEN engagement, Natasha is very ill, refusing to eat or drink. Eventually her unhappiness fades, though her former interests—flirting with men, in particular—have all but disappeared. The only person whom she is pleased to see is Pierre, who comes to visit and treats her very

tenderly. He never speaks of his
love for her. He is a married man,
after all, and she isn't even thinking
of such things anymore.

On the eve of the invasion,
Natasha ventures to church with
her family. She is deeply moved
by the service, and in addition to
praying for things like world peace
and happiness, she says a prayer for
Nikolai, regretful for the hurt she's
caused him.

SINCE THE NIGHT of Natasha's thwarted elopement, Pierre has changed, no longer feeling restless or wondering about the "meaning of it all." When his thoughts wander that way, they eventually rest on her, on Natasha. Instead of allowing himself to feel guilty about it, he tells himself, "I love her, and no one will ever know of it."

This love doesn't keep him from his usual ways of drinking and partying, though. He continues as before—he has to pass the time somehow. He does dine with the Rostovs every Sunday. One Sunday, when he arrives, Natasha is practicing her singing, for the first time since recovering from her illness.

At dinner, Petya, Natasha's younger brother of fifteen, announces his intention of joining the military, which his parents rebuff. Count Rostov asks Pierre why he never entered the army, to which Pierre replies that he wouldn't be any good at it. Pierre cuts the evening short and leaves earlier than usual. When Natasha runs after him, asking why he's not staying, he wants to blurt out that he's in love with her. But he merely kisses her hand and leaves, silently resolving not to return again.

FOR THE FIRST TIME, Tolstoy spends time with Petya, Natasha's younger brother, who's terribly disappointed at his parents' negative reaction to his desire to join the military. He sneaks out of the house to join the crowds awaiting the Tsar, who's expected to arrive at the Kremlin. When his carriage passes, the crowd surges, and Petya is jabbed and passes out. He comes to and manages to tussle with an elderly woman over a biscuit tossed out a window by the Tsar. Petya heads home, more resolved than ever to join the army the next day.

Count Rostov sets about to find a position for him that involves the least likelihood of his getting hurt.

PIERRE JOINS HIS FELLOW noblemen at a gathering convened by the Tsar. Before the Tsar arrives, they wonder why it is they've been summoned, passions rising. In an impassioned speech, a tearful Tsar tells the men—also in tears—that the time has come to act. The men, so moved, express their willingness to give everything they have to the purpose of defending their country.

❧❧

TOLSTOY ADDRESSES the conflicting accounts of what led to Napoleon's defeat. He argues that the Russians—contrary to what many Russian historians claim—did not retreat with the express intention of luring the ill-equipped

French deep into the country with winter around the corner. Tolstoy calls it "fortuitous" that Napoleon followed the Russian troops all the way to Moscow, unprepared for such a long engagement or the harsh Russian winter.

In any case, it's time to check in with Marya, who's being blamed by her father for causing Andrei's hasty departure from Bald Hills—even though it's his own fault. Poor saint Marya.

Luckily, shortly after leaving, Andrei writes to his father and asks forgiveness, which softens the old prince's heart. He even pushes Mademoiselle Bourienne away. In another letter, Andrei urges his father to move everyone to Moscow. Bald Hills is right on the path Napoleon is taking, and it's not safe there. The old prince is very flighty, though, and pays no attention to Andrei's warning. And so Marya sends one of her stewards, Alpatych, to travel to the town of Smolensk to deliver a letter to the governor asking for his input, if he thinks they are in danger at Bald Hills.

People are fleeing Smolensk. The governor tells Alpatych to urge Marya and her father to leave for the safety of Moscow, where he, himself, is heading. But before Alpatych can head back to Bald Hills, the village comes under fire. Alpatych heads down to the inn's cellar, where he hides with several others while, "the whistle of shells, and the piteous moaning of the cook, which rose above the hubbub, never ceased for an instant." By dusk, a hush has fallen over the town, though smoke remains. Alpatych ventures out of the cellar, "and through this smoke, gleaming strangely high in the sky, stood the sickle of the new moon." The day is August 6, 1812.

On his way back to Bald Hills, Alpatych runs into Andrei, who quickly scribbles an urgent note to his sister to leave for Moscow, as the French are only about a week out from arriving there. The town burns and is abandoned.

IT IS AUGUST 10, and Andrei is marching with his regiment past the road that leads to Bald Hills. Thankfully he knows that his family is no longer there—they left a couple of days ago for Moscow.

Still, there is plenty else to be worried about, including the shape of his regiment. He does take a quick detour to the estate but finds it nearly empty, save for Alpatych, who has remained. Andrei advises him to leave and then catches back up with his regiment.

In fact, Marya is not on her way to Moscow. The old prince has suffered a debilitating stroke, and so they have left for Bogucharovo, another of the family's country estates, where they stay for a while, the prince practically in a coma, neither improving nor getting worse. Soon it becomes dangerous for them to stay where they are. The French are practically on all sides of them.

They prepare to depart on August 15, but the prince takes a turn for the worse. He is able to speak and apologize to his daughter before suffering a second, fatal stroke. Marya is devastated, of course.

Alpatych urges Marya to leave for Moscow, though she feels she can't leave her father. Mademoiselle Bourienne (*who's French!*) shows Marya a French flyer promising protection of any citizens who remain in their homes. This awakens Marya out of her stupor of grief. To willingly give in to French control? She can't possibly stay!

She finds out that the peasants are starving and orders that all of the estate's grain be given to them. The peasants, however, for the most part have become French sympathizers and refuse to accept it—despite being hungry. Marya does not understand at all but plans to leave the next morning.

AT THIS POINT, Bogucharovo is about halfway between the French and Russian camps. Nikolai has set out from the Russian camp to a nearby village to seek hay for the horses.

Alpatych sees that Nikolai is an officer and asks for his help since the peasants aren't allowing Marya to leave Boguchavoro. Nikolai can't believe this to be the truth. After Marya tells him what's happened and begs for his help to leave, Nikolai promises he will escort her off the property himself.

Nikolai goes off to give the peasants a real tongue-lashing. Within a couple of hours, the carts are in front of the house, ready to take Marya away to Moscow. As promised, Nikolai accompanies her to the end of the Russian encampment. She thanks him profusely. He says he hopes to meet her again under better circumstances.

Once alone, Marya wonders whether she might be in love with her brave savior. As for Nikolai, he, too, imagines marrying Marya: "to think of her made him happy." But he's promised Sonya that he will marry her once the war is over. Seems like a love triangle might be brewing.

❦

KUTUZOV HAS ORDERED Andrei to report to headquarters. While waiting to meet with Kutuzov, Andrei meets Denisov, who's also waiting. Andrei knows of Denisov, since Natasha has told him about all of her suitors, which include the earnest lieutenant colonel. Andrei and Denisov each inwardly feel stabs of pain at remembering their follies with the young girl.

Kutuzov tells Andrei that he would like for him to work on his staff. Andrei says he rather likes his regiment and hopes to stay with them.

❧

WITH THE AMOUNT of frivolity happening in Moscow at this time, it's as if the residents aren't aware that the French are closing in on the city. They are aware, but it doesn't stop the partying.

Pierre runs into Julie, who's having trouble with the recent ban on speaking French (speak the traitorous language and pay a fine). Julie relates how Marya has just arrived in town, including her rescue by Nikolai. Julie also lets Pierre know that there are rumors swirling of his own interest in Natasha, to which he protests that he hasn't been to see the Rostovs in more than a month.

Soon, everyone starts leaving Moscow, worried the French will eventually make it there. Pierre remains, as do the Rostovs. After seeing a French cook being flogged, accused of being a spy, Pierre becomes so overwhelmed by the injustice of it all that he finally decides, once and for all, to join the army. Passing through the Russian camps, seeing all of the troops,

Pierre feels a surge of excitement, anticipation, and purpose.

Tolstoy describes the battles of Shevardino and Borodino—both how they've been inaccurately portrayed in history and how they really went down.

It's August 25, 1812, and Pierre wanders through the Russian camps. He runs into Boris, who asks what he's doing there. Pierre replies that he'd like to take in the view of the battle. (Apparently he's had time

to rethink his notion of joining.)
Boris proposes to show Pierre
around. The militiamen are putting
on clean white shirts to prepare for
the battle the next day.

Kutuzov spots Pierre and calls
him over. He compliments Pierre's
wife—the beautiful Ellen—and
offers his quarters to Pierre.
Dolokhov runs up to Pierre,
embraces him, and apologizes for
the years-ago "misunderstanding"
between them (over Ellen—that

led to the duel). Pierre doesn't know what to say.

Then, Pierre is taken on a tour of the line, which he is most anxious to see.

❦

ON THAT EVE OF THE BATTLE, Andrei is restless, contemplating the impending fight, his nerves, life and death, lost love, his departed father, and other such matters. He is annoyed by the arrival of Pierre and launches into something of a tirade against the "civility" of war. There should be no prisoners—they should fight to kill or be killed. He feels it's his last meeting with Pierre, who dismisses Andrei's behavior as mere pre-battle nerves.

Andrei is unable to sleep that night, reflecting on one particular conversation he had with Natasha. His thoughts drift to Anatol, which gets his blood boiling.

MEANWHILE, IN THE FRENCH
camp, on the eve of the battle, Napoleon yells to his generals, "No prisoners!" Napoleon also predicts their
arrival in Moscow in three days' time.
The emperor is presented with a portrait of his new son. Tolstoy describes
Napoleon's reaction to the portrait
as self-conscious and calculated, pre-
senting him as aware of the historical
significance of the moment.

Napoleon draws up his orders for the battle, which are impressive but not realistic. Indeed, Napoleon will be so far from the battle the next day that he won't even know how it unfolds.

❧❧

DESPITE THE RATTLING cannon shots, Pierre does not stir in the morning and has to be awoken by a groom. Everyone else has left. The battle has begun.

From his distant vantage point, Pierre surveys the battlefield, in awe of what's unfolding. He climbs on top of one of his horses and follows one of the generals heading toward the battlefield, wanting to experience it for himself. He loses the general, though, and ends up in the middle of a battalion, with soldiers sending him dirty looks for adding being trampled by a horse to the list of dangers they have to worry about. Pierre finds himself in the thick of battle.

Napoleon's troops are losing and fleeing. He ends up ordering a retreat.

❧

A CANNONBALL LANDS near Andrei—whose regiment has been ordered to stand by during the battle—and he is severely injured in his abdomen. He's whisked away to the medical tent, where, floating in and out of consciousness, he notices a man around whom every-

one's making a fuss. After the man's
leg is amputated, Andrei finally
realizes who he is: Anatol Kuragin.
Andrei is flooded with memories
of Natasha and feels such a strong
sense of compassion for Anatol,
which he attributes to the influence
of his recent acquaintance, the
saintly Marya.

WHILE THE BATTLE is not exactly
a win for the Russians—who lose

way more men than the French—
they stand their ground and don't
allow Napoleon to advance any
closer to Moscow. The tide has
turned, it seems.

That said, the Russians—suffering great losses after Borodino—do eventually continue
their retreat, all the way back to
Moscow (and beyond), the French
on their heels. When the French
reach Moscow, they stay there for
five weeks.

Tolstoy points out that Kutuzov does not take his decision to abandon Moscow to the French lightly. He considers it a necessity, though historians criticize him harshly for it. Kutuzov sees Russia's salvation in its army, which he feels needs to retreat from the city in order to regroup.

LET'S BACK UP A LITTLE, and turn to Countess Ellen. She's been carrying on affairs with two men, an older member of the Tsar's court and a younger prince. Unable to decide between the two of them, she tells both that the only way they can have any sway over her is by marrying her.

Um, since she's already married to Pierre, remember, she converts to Catholicism. You see, the Catholic Church won't recognize a marriage that's conducted within the confines of a "false religion." She settles on

the younger prince and writes to
Pierre asking for a divorce.

AFTER THE BATTLE, Pierre
wanders about, more than a
little shell-shocked. When he's
approached by some soldiers and
offered food, he lies about who he
is, not wanting to reveal his nobility. His groom finds him, blowing
his cover, which elicits a little teas-
ing from the soldiers.

With no room at the inn, Pierre spends the night in his carriage. During his restless sleep, he dreams of an old benefactor, who tells him that "Man can have dominion over nothing so long as he fears death, but he who fears it not possesses all." Pierre is greatly affected by these words. In the morning, he proceeds to Moscow, arriving a few days later.

In Moscow, Pierre reads the letter from his wife, in which she claims that Anatol and Andrei are dead and that she wants a divorce. Then, in an utterly timeless act, "without undressing, [Pierre] went to his bed, threw himself down on it, and instantly fell asleep." In the morning, he leaves the house through the back gates and disappears into the city.

EVEN THOUGH THE ARRIVAL of the French is imminent, the Rostovs are still in Moscow, waiting first for Petya's return from militia training and then for their belongings to be packed up. In fact, their belongings take up an astounding thirty carriages.

Sonya is feeling glum because the last letter from Nikolai to the family positively gushed over Marya, prompting the countess to giddily predict a marriage between them. Poor Sonya realizes Marya is a better match for Nikolai, but of

course her heart still hurts at
the prospect of not marrying
him herself.

Things are getting rough in the
city, with mobs rioting and the
police having already left town.
The Rostovs quickly finish packing
and prepare to leave in the morning. Meanwhile, they allow injured
soldiers to be brought into the
house. One of them, who arrives
during the night, turns out to be a
familiar face: It is Andrei!

The next morning, Berg shows up at the house. He's now a lieutenant. Of course, everyone wants to know the latest news from the battlefield. He recounts how brave the Russians were against the French at Borodino.

The count is asked if he might transport some of the wounded in his carriages. He agrees, but upon learning that this will mean their valuables will be left behind, the countess orders him to take back

his promise. Natasha gets wind of
this and blows up at her mother for
being so cruel as to leave the men
behind. The countess relents, and
so they start unloading the carts
of possessions and replacing them
with the men.

Sonya discovers that Andrei
is among the wounded they're
transporting and that he's dying.
The countess says Natasha must
not know. On their way out of the
city, they recognize Pierre walk-

ing through the streets, wearing a coachman's coat, looking very serious and distracted. He says hello but is clearly not himself.

The Rostovs continue on their journey, but we remain with Pierre. In the two days since he disappeared from his own house, Pierre has disguised himself as a peasant and acquired a pistol.

ON SEPTEMBER 2, Napoleon reaches the outskirts of Moscow and orders his troops to advance. He is disappointed and affronted when he learns that the city has been evacuated, the Russian army nowhere to be found. He was hoping for at least a little struggle.

COUNT ROSTOPCHIN has remained in Moscow, with instructions to maintain public order as best he can, a role that he embraces with enthusiasm. When he's told to evacuate, he feels unappreciated and annoyed that all of his efforts are for naught. He orders all prisoners and "lunatic asylum" patients released into the streets. With one exception: He orders that a political prisoner named Vereshchagin be brought to him.

An angry mob has formed outside Rostopchin's house. They are ready to take on the French,

hungry for a fight. Rostopchin offers Vereshchagin to them, "the scoundrel who has brought about the ruin of Moscow!" Rostopchin tells the crowd that the political prisoner had aligned himself with the French. The crowd, already blood-thirsty, becomes a mob and proceeds to beat Vereshchagin to death.

Trying to stem his guilt, Rost-opchin reasons with himself that Vereshchagin had already been

---

NAPOLEON WATCHES AS MOSCOW BURNS.

sentenced to death and that the crowd needed to be appeased. In the end, he believes that he has "killed two birds with one stone"—or one person, anyway. In the end, though, it's clear that his conscience will haunt him.

❧

THE FRENCH TROOPS arrive in Moscow, and finding it empty (for the most part), proceed to set up camp in the deserted mansions.

There are so many provisions and comforts that they just sort of make themselves at home, even though they've been ordered not to. In effect, the French army has disbanded: the soldiers "were absorbed into it [Moscow] like water into sand."

PIERRE IS STILL IN MOSCOW, staying at the home of his Masonic mentor, who's passed away. Also at the house is Makar, his mentor's brother, who is elderly and not in his right mind.

Pierre is having trouble processing everything he witnessed at Borodino, feeling insignificant compared to the soldiers who so bravely fought against the French. All of this leads up to his reckless decision to find Napoleon and assassinate him. Lacking sleep and drinking too much—in addition to obsessing over his plan—have left him in a bad way.

Some French soldiers arrive at the house, and Pierre manages to prevent one of them from being shot by Makar, who's gotten ahold of Pierre's pistol. The French soldier thanks Pierre for saving his life and pronounces Pierre a "Frenchman," not paying attention when Pierre tries to explain that he's Russian.

Pierre and the Frenchman (Captain Ramballe) chat throughout dinner, about the war, women, and Napoleon, whom Ramballe says is due to make his grand entrance into Moscow the next day. Whether it's the wine talking or his being touched by Ramballe's sincere offer of friendship, Pierre ends up spilling the details of his whole life. Pierre falls asleep as soon as his head hits the pillow.

THE ROSTOVS SETTLE IN for the night in a village outside of

Moscow. Sonya has told Natasha that Andrei is among the wounded traveling with them.

Andrei has a horrific wound to his abdomen, and the doctor knows that he will not survive, that, in fact, his death will be very painful. In his delirium, Andrei recalls his love for Natasha, regretting his harsh rejection of her. Suddenly, she appears before him—she's snuck out of bed to find him.

She immediately asks for forgiveness, to which he says he loves
her more than he ever has. From
that moment on, Natasha doesn't
leave Andrei's side.

IT'S SEPTEMBER 3, 1812. Pierre
wakes up with a hangover and "a
vague sense of having done something shameful the day before."
Oh yeah, he spilled his guts to
Ramballe. But never mind, it's

time for him to execute his plan to execute Napoleon.

When Pierre ventures into the Moscow streets, he sees that there are several fires burning, with no one seemingly attempting to extinguish them. The streets are empty, and gates are locked up. He comes upon a family, the mother weeping loudly. They've just escaped a fire, but their three-year-old daughter didn't make it out.

Pierre follows one of the children back to the house and finds the little girl hiding in the garden. He tries to take her back to her family, but they aren't where he left them. Someone else recognizes the girl, though, and Pierre hands her over to be delivered back to her parents.

Pierre becomes distracted by a very beautiful Armenian girl who's being questioned (with her family) by a couple of French soldiers. When one of the soldiers rips the necklace from the girl's neck, Pierre leaps forward, demanding that he stop. Next thing he knows, he's fighting the soldier. His weapon is discovered, and the jig is up. He's arrested as an "incendiary."

ঌ BOOK IV ঌ

M EANWHILE, BACK IN Petersburg, you'd never know that a war is going on. Society continues as it always has, with balls and dinners and plays. Tolstoy backs up to August 26, the day of the battle at Borodino. That evening, Anna Pavlovna is having one of her soirees. Of much discussion is the fact that Ellen has missed quite a few functions—she's fallen ill with angina.

The next day, word arrives from Kutuzov supposing that Borodino was a Russian victory. It's hardly a decisive outcome, but the people of Petersburg rejoice anyway. Ellen, who's received no word from Pierre about her request for a divorce, takes an overdose and dies a very painful death, which puts a shadow over the city. Then, when word of the French invasion of Moscow comes, well, everyone's just down-right depressed.

NIKOLAI IS SENT to Voronezh to rustle up some supplies for his regiment. He meets with the governor, who claims that his wife is a good friend of Nikolai's mother. The governor invites Nikolai over to a soiree that evening. There, Nikolai is delighted to find "an inexhaustible number of young married ladies and pretty girls impatiently awaiting his attention." The one he latches onto for the night happens to be a pretty blonde who's married. Her husband doesn't appreciate all of the attention Nikolai is paying to his wife.

It turns out that Marya's aunt is also at the party. Nikolai is introduced to her and then confides in the governor's wife about his dilemma: his promise of marriage to Sonya and his feeling that fate somehow brought him and Marya together. Marya, it so happens, is staying with her aunt in Petersburg at the moment.

A few days later, Nikolai calls on Marya and her aunt. The visit is brief, but they are both feeling (*so*

to speak!) and checking each other out. Nikolai is as conflicted as ever, having difficulty picturing himself married to Marya: "If he tried, it all seemed incongruous and false. It only made him uneasy."

Since she's still in mourning for her father, Marya is not allowed to go out, and Nikolai feels it would be wrong to court her in any way. Still, he's intrigued by her and, well, conflicted. One day, he receives a letter from Sonya in which she declares her love for him, along with her desire to not cause conflict within his family. And so she tells him to consider himself no longer bound to her.

When news of Andrei's injury reaches Marya, she decides to set out to find him. And Nikolai rejoins his regiment.

BEFORE THEY LEFT for Moscow, Nikolai's mother asked Sonya to promise that she would not hold him to any understanding they may have had. Sonya agreed to no such promise, though. She loves him so much and is determined not to let him go so easily.

In that era, in-laws were not allowed—legally—to marry. Had Andrei married Natasha before Natasha mucked things up, then Nikolai (as Natasha's brother) would not have been able to marry Marya (who was Andrei's sister).

So when Andrei showed up at the Rostovs' house, wounded, Sonya hatched a plan, hoping that love would once again bloom between him and Natasha. Sonya, for her part, doesn't consider herself a plan-hatcher. She merely believes that fate has intervened by bringing Andrei to the Rostovs' house, and that she and Nikolai are simply meant to be together.

Certain that her plan will work and that Natasha and Andrei's union will forbid one between Marya and Nikolai, Sonya gives in to the countess's request and writes to Nikolai telling him he is free to do as he wishes.

PIERRE IS BEING HELD by the French as an "incendiary." After going through a couple of interrogations, he is marched, along with five other prisoners, to a kitchen garden next to a convent. The five other men are executed by firing squad in one of the most harrowing scenes I've ever read. Though Pierre's life is spared, he feels numbed to life, his faith in humanity utterly destroyed.

Later, he is told that he's been pardoned (meaning, spared execution), but the words don't have particular meaning to him. He's transferred to a barracks, where an older prisoner named Platon Karatayev offers some of his potatoes to the famished Pierre, along with the sage observation: "suffer an hour, live an age." In other words, life goes on. And so Pierre feels a renewed sense of hope. Pierre spends a month imprisoned with Platon and twenty other men. It is Platon who makes a lasting impression on him.

❧

MARYA ARRIVES in Yaroslavl, where her brother Andrei is staying with the Rostovs. When she goes in to see him, she's shocked by his appearance. He looks like a man who's clearly accepted that death is near and inevitable.

Tolstoy walks us through Andrei's transformation from a wounded man who wants to live, to love, with hope; to a man who feels bitter when he realizes he won't get the chance to love Natasha as he wishes; to a man who feels somewhat free from the fear of death; to a man who's completely checked out, going through the motions that are expected of a dying man.

After it's all over, Natasha and Marya weep "out of a reverent emotion that filled their souls before the solemn mystery of a death that had been consummated in their presence."

❧❧

WITH THE FRENCH firmly ensconced in Moscow—pampered by its riches—and the Russian troops gaining strength and restocking supplies in Tarutino, Napoleon sends word to Kutuzov that he wishes to discuss terms for a peace agreement. Kutuzov replies that he wouldn't think of it.

All Kutuzov wants is for the French to get out of his country. Indeed, "the desire for revenge that lay in the heart of every Russian so long as the French were in Moscow" was practically palpable. There are some minor battles (skirmishes, really) between the French (small squadrons stationed on the outskirts of Moscow) and Russians, with the Russians victorious.

Tolstoy points out that, in Moscow, the French have arms and riches to easily wipe out the remaining Russian troops. But they don't. Instead, Napoleon and his troops stay in Moscow through October with apparently no thought of attempting to engage with the Russian troops.

Shortly after arriving in Moscow, Napoleon issues a proclamation of his intent to restore order to the city. He says that Russians can return to their jobs, their trades, their worship—all in peace. Only acts against the emperor or French troops will be punished. And his own troops will be punished, themselves, if caught pillaging or neglecting their military duties.

In reality, though, the promises in Napoleon's proclamation don't

really happen. More of Moscow
burns, with looting widespread;
there are no artisans left in the city;
and one priest attempting to carry
out Napoleon's wishes is slapped in
the face by a French soldier in the
middle of a service.

In October, Napoleon leaves
a small garrison in Moscow and
begins the retreat from Moscow,
both he and his men taking with
them a large amount of booty.

IT'S OCTOBER, and Pierre is still being held prisoner. Though the conditions are spare, there is no cruelty, and a camaraderie among the prisoners has developed. (The French have offered to move him to another shed, to be held in better conditions with other officers, but Pierre chooses to remain with his group.)

While outside his shed, Pierre notices the French troops parading by with their wagons of booty. It's been warm out considering the time of year—what we call "Indian summer," the Russians call "old wives' summer." Pierre finds out from one of the soldiers guarding them that the French are retreating and that word is expected shortly about what is to be done with the prisoners.

In the month that Pierre has been imprisoned, he has found the peace of mind he's been searching for his whole life. When he thinks of his plan to assassinate Napoleon, he can hardly believe that he ever considered doing such a thing. When he thinks of his wife, he feels nothing of the resentment he once felt. (He's not yet aware of her death.) The simple things in life—good sleep, adequate food, the freedom of choice—are all that he desires.

On October 6, Pierre and the other prisoners are herded along with the evacuating French troops.

Traveling through the streets of Moscow, they lament the state of their ravaged city. It is very slow-going, the streets clogged with soldiers and wagons loaded down with furs, icons, and other riches the French have stolen.

Everyone is cranky, except for the prisoners, who joke among themselves of the funny things they've seen during the march. In fact, Pierre goes off by himself, sits down, and bursts into laughter.

The others thinks he's a little loony, but he's just overcome by the absurdity of the whole situation. After his outburst, Pierre returns to his fellow prisoners and goes to sleep for the night.

❧

KUTUZOV IS STILL DOING everything he can to avoid going on the offensive: "Patience and time are my two valiant warriors." That said, he does lie awake at night going over and over the thousands of things that might happen next. When he's informed of the French leaving Moscow and heading west, he exclaims, "Russia is saved. I thank Thee, Lord!" His gamble has paid off.

❧❧

TOLSTOY POSITS that the reason behind Russia's victory against the French is its enormous "spirit." The French lack this strength of spirit, which—despite its size and abundance of supplies—leads to its downfall. That and the guerrilla warfare that occurs along the lines of the French retreat.

Two of the men leading these small attacks are none other than Denisov and Dolokhov. Denisov is awaiting word from Dolokhov regarding an attack they're coordinating when a couple of men arrive bearing a message from the general. One of the "men" is the young

Petya Rostov, whom Denisov recognizes instantly. Petya is alive with anticipation, eager to engage with the French.

Denisov is tired of waiting for Dolokhov to arrive and decides to engage the French without his help. That night, Petya expresses his desire to command "something," during the attack. To say he's an eager beaver would be an understatement.

Dolokhov arrives. Petya is fascinated by him, as he's heard stories

of his bravery in battle and cruelty to the enemy. Denisov shares
his plans for the next day with
Dolokhov, who says they must get
a closer look at the French that
night. He proposes to put on a
French uniform and infiltrate the
camp. He asks Denisov for a man
to accompany him, and of course
Petya volunteers.

The two put on uniforms,
mount their horses, and ride over
to the French camp. Dolokhov

asks where the officers are and is directed to them. Speaking in French, Dolokhov explains that he and Petya are on their own, trying to catch up to a regiment ahead of them. Dolokhov gets tons of information out of the French officers, who, if they're suspicious, certainly don't show it. Petya stays quiet the entire time, practically holding his breath and expecting the French to figure them out at any minute.

On their way back, Petya expresses his utter and complete awe of Dolokhov, even embracing him. Dolokhov is amused by the adoration and rides off into the night leaving Petya to return to Denisov on his own.

Petya, breathless with excitement, tells Denisov of what went down in the French camp. After Denisov falls asleep, Petya can't imagine sleeping, himself.

Morning arrives, and the Russians prepare for the attack. Denisov asks Petya to stay by his side no matter what, but Petya gets caught up in the excitement and charges ahead, on his own. His horse gallops through the action. He falls from his horse, a bullet through his skull in the least surprising death of the entire book.

One of the Russian prisoners rescued in the attack is none other than Pierre. At this point in the march, the number of Russian prisoners has diminished by two-thirds, due to illness, desertion, or being shot by the soldiers for lagging behind. The only way Pierre has been able to cope with his own physical discomfort and witnessing the atrocities around him has been by not thinking about them.

And so when Platon Karatayev fell ill, Pierre distanced himself, not allowing himself to be affected by his friend's suffering. Instead, he inwardly marveled at man's strength and ability to overcome hardship.

Basically, he willed himself into somewhat of a delusional state.

One morning, Pierre saw Karatayev propped up against a tree, with two French soldiers standing over him. Karatayev looked at Pierre with his "kindly round eyes, now veiled with tears," and Pierre turned away. Pierre heard the shot but did not allow himself to turn around for a look. He and his fellow prisoners continued forward on their march. It's a truly gut-wrenching scene.

When Denisov and Dolokhov storm the camp and free Pierre and his fellow prisoners, Pierre sobs with relief and joy, grabbing the first soldier who comes up to him and kissing him.

THE CONDITION of the French procession is worsening by the day. The weather is brutally cold; they are turning on each other, resorting to murder for food and supplies. Tolstoy sums it up as this: "Those who could get away did so, and those who could not—surrendered or died."

As for Napoleon, he has all but abandoned everyone, taking off for home all by himself. Tolstoy questions how in the world Napoleon could still be referred to as "grand" after such an act of cowardice and self-preservation. It is a mystery to him.

Despite its severely weakened state, the French army is not

obliterated by the Russians, who have trouble keeping up with the rapidly retreating French. Tolstoy points out that there was no real point in the Russians mounting a serious offensive on the French— after all, they were retreating, trying to get the hell out of Dodge as soon as they could. Plus, the Russian army was in a weakened state, itself. There were lots of reasons this didn't happen, but still, the Russians are criticized

by historians for this lack of an aggressive pursuit.

AFTER ANDREI'S DEATH, Marya and Natasha grieve on their own, not really discussing their profound loss. Marya, at least, has the distraction of now being the guardian to Andrei's young son, Nikolenka. She makes plans to return with him to Moscow. She invites Natasha to accompany them, but Natasha cannot bear to leave the place where she last was with Andrei.

Natasha continually goes over one of her last conversations with Andrei before he took a turn for the worse. He said that he didn't want to go on living in so much pain and agony. She agreed with him, seeing his point. Now, she deeply regrets having agreed with him, feeling her own pain at the loss of him unbearable. She imagines telling him that she loves him, which she never told him.

Suddenly news arrives of Petya's death, and all of the Rostovs are devastated, especially the countess who fluctuates between sobs, delirium, and denial. Natasha never leaves her mother's side for three weeks. She finds renewed strength in this tending to her mother, like it's given her a purpose, woken her from her grief over Andrei.

Still, the constant vigil and comforting takes a toll on Natasha's

own health. And so Marya tends to
Natasha, and a tender affection and
true friendship blossom between
them. And so, when Marya eventually leaves for Moscow, Natasha
accompanies her.

KUTUZOV IS UNABLE to prevent
the battle that takes place at Kras-
noe, in which the Russians pick
off the ailing, starving, freezing
French troops. Tens of thousands

of French are captured, along with cannons and other munitions. Kutuzov ventures into the camps, where he sees both the French and his own soldiers in a pretty sad state. He tells his men to hold on for just a little while longer: "We'll see our visitors off and then we'll rest. The Tsar won't forget your service." He also asks them to treat their prisoners with compassion. The men cheer when he's finished his rousing speech. Afterward,

Kutuzov breaks out into sobs.

There is much dissatisfaction regarding Kutuzov's accomplishments among those who believe that the Russians should do all they can to crush the French. Kutuzov is called to Vilna, where the Tsar is staying. The Tsar decorates Kutuzov and fetes him with a banquet but privately expresses his disappointment at some of his decisions. Kutuzov realizes his career is pretty much over.

The Tsar is not satisfied with just driving the French from Russia. He wants glory for Russia in the west, in liberating Europe from Napoleon. Because Kutuzov does not see the reason for doing anything beyond kicking the French out, all of Kutuzov's powers are transferred to the Tsar. With his job done, there's nothing left for Kutuzov to do aside from die. Which he does.

IT TAKES PIERRE three months after being freed to recover from his ordeal—physically, of course. The psychological effects of the war will remain with him the rest of his life. During his recovery, he learns of Andrei's death—even of Ellen's death for the first time. He feels at great peace, thankful for every little thing in his life, from a hot boullion to a clean bed.

Replacing his previous inner unrest is a newfound faith, faith that God is "here and every-where," and a comfort knowing that he need not consume his life with worrying about his philandering wife or the threat of the French. He is free. As a result of this change, he is generally better company—people want to talk to him, now that he actually listens to them.

After three months' time, Pierre decides it's time to return to Moscow, to help in the rebuilding efforts and pay off his wife's debts, which are great.

❧

AS SOON AS THE FRENCH depart from Moscow, Russians flood back into the city "as blood flows to the heart." When Pierre arrives there in January of 1813, he finds the city to be bursting with life and renewal. He is happy to see former acquaintances, as they are to see him. He maintains his distance, though, keeping his plans undefined and vague. When he hears that Marya is staying in the city, he goes to visit her, wanting to hear about his dear friend Andrei's last days.

Pierre speaks with Marya a good couple of minutes before he realizes that her gaunt, somber, dressed-in-black companion is none other than Natasha. Pierre feels his love for her renewed and a great deal of his freedom vanished, as he, for the first time, cares what someone else

(Natasha) is thinking of him. He asks about Andrei's final days, and Natasha opens up, sharing every detail leading up to his death, after which she flees the room, overcome by grief. Despite the drama, Marya invites Pierre to stay for dinner.

After dinner, Natasha and Marya express an interest in hearing from Pierre about everything he went through. And so he shares everything, including details he's never told anyone. It's three in the morning when he finishes and heads home. Afterward, Marya and Natasha have a pow-wow before going to bed, both marveling at what a wonderful man Pierre is, what a changed man.

The next day, Pierre decides that he will do anything to make Natasha his wife. He goes over to Marya's house again for dinner. After dinner when Natasha excuses herself for the night, Pierre asks Marya what she thinks his chances might be with

Natasha. She instructs him to give it a little time. She advises him to write to Natasha's parents and leave for Petersburg for a while. Marya will work on Natasha. Pierre leaves with elation at the thought that Natasha might soon be his.

Marya tells Natasha of her conversation with Pierre, which fills Natasha with hope and joy. She's annoyed to hear that he's left for Petersburg for a while but is looking forward to becoming his wife someday.

❧ EPILOGUE ❧

TOLSTOY REVISITS the notion of the fluidity and subjectivity of history, specifically in relation to the war and Tsar Alexander I. He argues that while history may appear to be composed of a series of chance occurrences, if we accept that the unfolding of world events is part of a grand design outside of our comprehension, then there is a certain amount of peace and acceptance that comes with it.

1813 BRINGS both joy and sadness to the Rostovs: Natasha and Pierre are married, but Natasha's father passes away, seemingly too aggrieved by the losses of Andrei and Petya and for making such a mess of the family's finances, the true extent of which becomes clear after his death. Nikolai is in Paris with the Russian army upon hearing the news and heads home to Moscow immediately. He takes on his father's enormous debts, wanting to restore the family's honor by paying them off.

After selling the entire estate and borrowing some from Pierre, Nikolai takes a civil servant position in the government and moves with his mother and Sonya to a house in the "poorer quarters" of Moscow, though Nikolai and Sonya do their best to keep the fact that they're now poor from the countess. Natasha and Pierre are living in Petersburg so aren't aware of just how dire the circumstances are, either.

Nikolai is impressed by Sonya's goodness and devotion to his mother, but he no longer loves her. The idea of marrying a wealthy woman just because she could make all of his troubles go away is repulsive. He just endures his situation as best he can.

WHEN MARYA VENTURES to Moscow for a visit, she calls on the Rostovs. Nikolai greets her very coldly, no doubt his pride wounded by his circumstances. The countess, however, won't shut up about the lovely Marya, bugging Nikolai to go call on her. He finally relents, just to appease her.

Their exchange is just as formal and awkward as the last time.

At the end of it, though, Marya
exclaims that she has so little happiness in her life that each loss—
including that of his friendship—is
especially hard on her. He softens a
bit, but she runs out of the room.

IN 1814, Nikolai and Marya
marry, and settle in at Bald Hills
with the countess and Sonya.
Within a few years, he's paid off
all of his debts and soon takes a

great interest in farming, especially in the lives of his peasants, striving to understand and take care of them.

❧

IT'S DECEMBER 5, 1820, and Natasha and her four children (three daughters and a son) have been staying at Bald Hills for nearly seven weeks, while Pierre has been in Petersburg. Denisov is also visiting, and many guests are expected the next day, which is Nikolai's name day.

Marya and Nikolai are generally a happy couple, though he can be irritable and a little bossy. Natasha and Pierre are utterly devoted to one another, their whole lives revolving around their family. Natasha even nurses her own children, which is unheard of for nobility back then.

Pierre and Nikolai have a discussion about politics. Pierre has been in Petersburg to meet with a secret society of noblemen who disagree with how the country is being run. The whole idea of such a society doesn't sit well with Nikolai, who believes that a man's duty is first and foremost to his country, no matter what. Pierre and Nikolai are like water and oil, one man concerned with ideas and thought, the other with farming and order. That said, their wives love them for exactly who they are.

The section closes with Niko-lenka waking from a dream in which he feels the comforting caresses of his father, whom he can't remember. He strives to be a good man whom his father would have been proud of.

IN THE SECOND PART of the epilogue, we have bid adieu to all of our favorite characters. Tolstoy closes the book with additional philosophical musing on the concepts of history, free will, necessity, and power and how God factors into them. It's beautifully written and reasoned, but the section is a little boring—you should be very thankful that I've read it for you. Still, it doesn't diminish the greatness of this magnificent epic that I hope someday you might consider reading—though, be warned, it will take more than one sitting!

This book has been bound using handcraft methods and Smyth-sewn to ensure durability.

Designed by Susan Van Horn.

Written by Joelle Herr.

Edited by Jennifer Leczkowski.

The text was set in Adobe Garamond and PF Monumenta Pro.